THE GREAT RUBENS WORKSHOP

Catherine de Duve

KATE'ART
EDITIONS

Merchant ships come from all parts of the world to moor alongside the quays of Antwerp, the biggest port in Europe. Here they unload their precious cargoes: spices, cane sugar, silk, linen cloth, iron, copper, gold, diamonds, pigments…

In those days, Belgium did not yet exist as it was part of a region known as the Low Countries. The kings of Europe were fighting among themselves to share the world between them and battle raged between the Catholics and the Protestants. An eighty year war (1568-1648) had started. The City of Antwerp was also under threat… But happily in 1609 the Archdukes Albert and Isabella signed a twelve year peace agreement…

DAY

This is the golden age of Antwerp. You can find everything you want. You run into scholars, scientists and famous artists.

I'm from Africa!

Look at Antwerp harbour. What kind of ship is moored there? Where do the ships hail from? What are the houses like?

PETER PAUL RUBENS was born on June 28th 1577 in Siegen, in Germany. His father was a protestant lawyer and deputy mayor of Antwerp. One day he had to flee on account of the war with Spain and religious problems. So Rubens spent his childhood in Cologne. On the death of his father, the family returned to Antwerp as the situation had changed. The Spanish had reconquered the city and the Rubens family could once again settle in but on one condition which was to become Catholics.

At school, Peter Paul learned Latin, Flemish and French. While still a child he enjoyed drawing and made copies of illustrations he found in the bible. Later, he acquired the most beautiful works edited by his classroom friend Balthasar Moretus, the grandson of Plantin the famous printer.

Young Rubens was engaged as a page by a Countess before being articled, at the age of 15, to a landscape painter and then to the most famous artist in Antwerp, Otto Van Veen, who advised him to go to Italy to perfect his training. At about the age of 21, Rubens was appointed Master at the guild of St. Luke.

Balthasar Moretus

*A **Guild** is a grouping of artisans, merchants or artists who practise the same profession such as crossbowmen, fishermen, painters and the like…*

Like Rubens, learn to draw from an illustration in a book. Complete the drawing of the cat.

IN ITALY...

Michelangelo

Here we go, on the road to the country of art... In 1660, Rubens was 23 years old when he left for Italy, a real school for painters! For eight years, he discovered the sculptures of Roman antiquity and was inspired by the colours of the best known Venetian artists and of the *Italian renaissance*. Why are colours so much more beautiful in Venice? The light there is so special! There too you can find the most beautiful pigments in the world which are used to prepare the colours.

The Italian Renaissance: *After the Middle Ages, Italy is reborn as it rediscovers Antiquity and its art. Italy becomes an art centre thanks to its artists of genius such as Leonardo da Vinci (who painted the Mona Lisa), Michelangelo (who painted the Sistine Chapel), Titian...*

Observe the preparation of pigments: *coloured powder obtained their paint. Painters of old mixed these with a binding agent such as linseed*

| Root | Crushing | Pigments | + | Linseed oil and essences | = | Oil paint |

Titian

At the court of the Duke of Mantoua churches, Rubens painted portraits, copied paintings and decorated churches. In March 1603, he accompanied a convoy which was transporting presents for Philip III, the King of Spain, to Madrid. Now he's an ambassador! He meets the king and discovers his art collection which included works by Titian which he copies.

Compare the painting by Titian with that of Rubens. Search for Venetian colours on the palette.

from stones, roots, earth to make oil or a white of egg…

 # BEAUTY

Three beauties appear to be circling in a garden of paradise. They are "The Three Graces", daughters of Jupiter: Euphrosyne, Aglaea and Thalia. In Greek mythology, they are the guardians of the golden apples of the Hesperides garden.

What beauties! What do they represent?

Euphrosyne ("Mirth"), Aglaé ("Beauty") and Thalia ("Good Cheer").

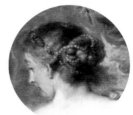

Rubens created his own ideal model. He described his vision of the human form as *"Solid flesh, firm and white, tainted by a pale red tone..., a gracious face, devoid of wrinkles, fleshy..., stomach and calves with a soft and flowing contour..., round, ample, snow-white and firm buttocks. Ample thighs... Small feet, delicate fingers and beautiful hair"*.

Now it's your turn. Draw Rubens' ideal model. But watch out; make sure you follow the master's advice.

BAROQUE

Church

While in Rome, Rubens took an interest in the new artistic movement known as *Baroque*. After the religious wars, the Catholics built ever bigger and more beautiful churches than before in a grandiose, theatrical and monumental style. The general public has to be impressed and amazed to ensure it remains Catholic. The new churches must be decorated. Who better than Rubens to realise the huge paintings of more than five metres in height?

The word Baroque derives from the Portuguese "Barroco" meaning "irregular pearl" which explains the irregular and highly ornate shapes of this art style.

Never had such impressive paintings been seen before! In paintings, the Baroque style loves to be an expression of emotions and movement which are depicted by spirals, oblique lines and strong lighting... Do you see how they lead our gaze?

Observe the composition of a Baroque painting.

THE THREE WISE MEN

Once upon a time, there was a star which shone so brightly in the sky that three wise men from the Orient, Balthasar, Melchior and Gaspard, recognised it. They knew that it would lead them to Jesus, the son of God. And so they crossed deserts and faraway countries with their caravans.

Then one day they saw that the star had stopped moving over Bethlehem in Judea. They were overcome with joy.

The Three Wise Men went into a small stable where a child wrapped in swaddling clothes lay sleeping in the manger beside his parents. They prostrated themselves before the infant King and adored Him. They then unpacked their treasures and offered Him their priceless gifts reserved only for Kings: gold, frankincense and myrrh. Do you see them?

Reposition the details in the painting and find the odd one out among the pieces of the puzzle.

RUBENS

At the age of 32, Rubens' reputation was made! He was named "Painter of the house of their highnesses", Archduke Albert and his wife, the infante Isabella, the sovereigns of the Low Countries established in Brussels. Rubens, who stayed in Antwerp, married Isabelle Brandt, aged 18 years of age. They were to have three children, Clara Serena, Albert and Nicholas.

How are Rubens and Isabella dressed at home?

HOUSE

Infante Isabella

A year later, Rubens bought a house in the Wapper, at that time the smartest part of Antwerp. He converted his house into a genuine Renaissance palace! He created a garden in antique style ornamented with sculptures conceived by him and representing Greek gods and he added a pavilion which is connected to the house by a portico. This is the big workshop. But what goes on in there?

Observe the interior of Rubens House. Find his self portrait, the still life, the Cordova leather and the furniture.

IN THE WORKSHOP

Here we go with orders! The ambitious Rubens set up a workshop which was designed to produce a great deal of paintings. After all, that's what the Italians did before him! Like them, he engaged students and young collaborators with talent. He trained them in his techniques and his style. Rubens was strict. He only kept the best. His reputation was at that price. It was necessary to work fast and well.

Take a close look at the different stages used by Rubens in this sketch called "modello":

| Joined planks | A preparatory layer of a white mixture based on chalk and animal glue | Tinted oil-based primer | "Modello", yellow ochre sketch |

White preparatory layer to obtain a smooth surface on the wooden plank.

Thickening of the oil paint being Rubens' last touch. The thicker layer permits the capture of light and creates volume.

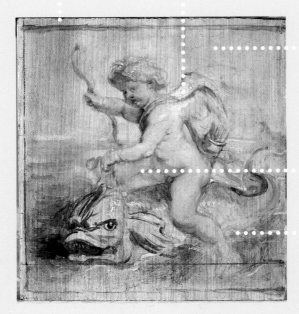

Impression layer: ochre-coloured paint applied with large strokes of the brush to give an overall basis.

Modello (the drawing): the outline of the characters and objects are traced rapidly in a dark ochre colour.

Glazing. This consists of fine, transparent colours to emphasise shading.

WITH FOUR HANDS

Van Dyck painted by Rubens

Everybody wants a Rubens for his parochial church, his guild company, his corporation or his brotherhood. There is no shortage of orders. But how can one paint so many paintings at the same time? In the 17th century it was common practice to paint a canvas assisted by one's pupils, leaving the finishing touches to the master or by executing them with four hands. This was known as collaboration. The two masters would then both sign the painting. Each one would paint those parts which he did best…

In your opinion, who painted this painting with Rubens? Jordaens, Van Dyck, "Velvet" Brueghel or Snijders?

JACOB JORDAENS (1593-1678) when he started he occasionally worked as an assistant with Rubens.

ANTOON VAN DYCK (1599-1641) was, from 1617 to 1620, chief assistant of Rubens who called him "the best of my pupils". This portrait artist of genius managed to copy the master's style to perfection. In 1620, the talented Van Dyck left Antwerp for London where he became the painter accredited to the court of the King of England.

JAN BRUEGHEL I THE ELDER (1568-1625) son of Pieter Bruegel the Elder. He painted the likes of flowers, of jewellery and of material objects with such love and affection that he was nicknamed "Velvet" Brueghel.

FRANS SNIJDERS (1579-1657) son of Pieter Brueghel the Elder. He painted the likes of flowers, of jewellery and of material objects with such love and affection that he was nicknamed "Velvet" Brueghel.

THE ART COLLECTION

In Rubens' day there were no museums. Art was to be found in the churches or in the house of rich collectors. While Rubens painted religious subjects, he also realised other subjects on smaller formats to decorate drawing rooms, or formal salons or to complete the collections of art and other works of interest.

Rubens' friend, Cornelis van der Geest, was an art dealer. He would place an order for a painting by an artist which he would then place in his catalogue, a sort of comprehensive book, which enabled him to show his collection in the four corners of the earth. "Come and admire my collection! Canvases by Rubens, Van Dyck, Brueghel. What treasures! What variety!" He says to his distinguished visitors, Archdukes Albert and Isabella, surrounded by courtesans and maids of honour.

Come and visit the Cornelis art collection and observe:

1. Where am I in the Cornelis collection?

2. Single out all that he collects: *Paintings, sculptures, coins, scientific instruments, shells, curiosities…*

3. Discover the different types of painting: *Portraits, mythological, allegorical, hunting scenes, landscapes, still life paintings, subject pictures…*

THEATRE

After settling into his new workshop in 1615, Rubens developed a theatrical baroque style. He portrayed a world which is in tumult, forever in movement, without any limits, intense and dramatic.

The characters portrayed show their feelings in an expressive way. You can read everything on their faces.

What expressions! Search for these emotions in the characters depicted: *Fear, anger, serenity, sadness, pride, joy, boredom, ire, terror...*

FAMILY

Rubens and his first wife Isabella

Rubens was knighted by Charles I, King of England. The artist was also a clever diplomat. Discreet, friendly and persuasive, he undertook secret missions for the crowned heads of Europe. Thanks to his profession as a painter he was able to conduct intimate conversations with kings. After the death of his wife, Rubens got married again - to Helen Fourment. He was 53 while she was barely 16 years of age... She was the daughter of a dealer in silk and tapestries. Helen was reputed to be "the most beautiful woman in Antwerp." She bore him four further children. Rubens, soft and attentive, liked to paint them at all ages... What a lovely family!

"I have decided to get married... I have chosen someone who will not be embarrassed at seeing me paintbrush in hand."

Look at Helen's wedding dress.

# ANIMALS

In the days of Rubens, hunting was a pastime appreciated by the nobility. Rubens executed a number of hunting scenes for them. These included tiger, lion, crocodile and hippopotamus hunts… Other animals, both wild and domestic, were to be seen in the paintings of the grand master, some of which turned into real Noah's arks.

 Draw a Noah's ark which shows your favourite animals. Get inspiration from those painted for or by Rubens and find their names.

MYTHOLOGY

Rubens received a large order from Marie de Medici, the Queen of France. She requested him to personally execute the decoration of one of the galleries at the Luxemburg Palace in Paris. In barely three years, from 1622 to 1625, he completed 25 large paintings. More than 300 square metres of canvas retrace the life of Marie and her husband Henry IV in an original way. The sovereigns are depicted as gods of mythology. Can you recognise them?

Find the characters in the painting. What have they become?

The town of Lyon: It is represented by a woman seated in a chariot pulled by two lions. This is an allegory, a person representing a town.

Jupiter and Juno: The king and the queen-mother have become gods. King Henry is Jupiter seated on an eagl while Marie is Juno beside her peacocks.

The hymen: The woman holding the torch symboli marriage and is accompanied by three young persons als holding a torch.

The putti : these are small winged angels like chubby babies. Seated astride two lions, they brandish torches to the glory of the royal couple.

ANGELS

An angel goes by… Avenging angels, striking bandits with thunder, or little puttis with plump flesh… Rubens loves to paint these chubby babies. Can you see them swimming in the clouds?

Search for the angels in the painting. How many are there? What are they doing?

Who is neither a putti nor an angel? Find the odd character. Discover the whole variety of wings which Rubens created for his little angels.

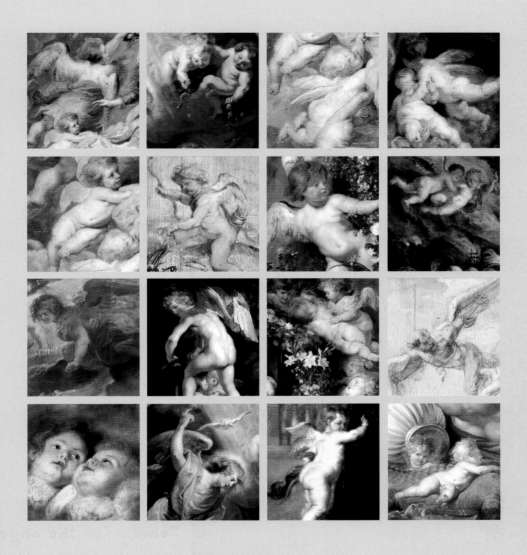

Eventually, Rubens, the master painter, died, rich and famous, in his Antwerp house on May 30th 1640 at the age of 62.

Texts and illustrations: Catherine de Duve - **Graphics:** Kate'Art Editions
Conception and creation: Kate'Art Editions & Happy Museum! - **Translation:** Roland King

ANTWERP:

Royal Museum of Fine Arts Antwerp (KMSKA) - Rubens:
Christ Crucified between the Two Thieves ('The Lance'), c.
1619-20: p.10, 22 - *The Adoration of the Magi, 1624:*
p.12-13, 22 - The Battle of the Amazons, c.1618-20: p.21-
Adam and Eve (detail), before 1600: cover p. 26 - **Snijders:**
Pantry with dog, monkey and parrot, towards 1640-1657: p.19 -
Jan Brueghel I: *Flowers in a vase,* (beginning of 17th century):
p.19 - **The Rubens House - Rubens:** *Self-Portrait,* c.1630:
p.1, 4 - *The Leganés Annunciation* (detail), before 1628: p.5,
27,31 *Portrait of Archduke Albert,* 1616-17 or later: p.14 -
*Portrait of Archduchess Isabelle,*1616-17 or later: p.15: - *Portrait
of Antoon van Dyck,* towards1615-16: p.18 - **Bonnecroy:** *View
of Antwerp,* 1658: p.2-3 - **Van Haecht:** *The Picture Gallery of
Cornelis van der Geest,* 1628: p.20-21 - **Harrewyn** copy after
J. Van Croes, *View of the Rubenshuis,* 1692: p.16
Photo: *The dining room in Rubens'house:* p.15
Plantin-Moretus Museum - Erasmus II Quellinus: *Portrait of
Balthazar I Moretus* for the engraver Cornelis Galle: p.5
Our Lady's Cathedral -Rubens: *The Assumption of the Holy
Virgin,* 1625-26: p.7, 22, 30-31

BRUSSELS:

**Royal Museums of Fine Arts of Belgium (MRBAB) -
Rubens:** *Four Negro Heads:* p.3- *The Carrying of the Cross,*
1636-37: p.11, 22 - *Cupid astride a dolphin:* p.17, 31 - *Portrait
of Paracelse:* p.21 - *The Martyrdom of St. Lieven,* ca.1636-37:
cover, p. 22-23, 30 - *The Fall of Icarus,* 1636: p.31 -
The Crowning of the Holy Virgin: p.31 - *Portret of Helena
Fourment:* cover - **Van Dyck:** *Portrait of Porzia Imperiale with
her Daughter Maria Francesca,* ca.1623: p.19 - **Jordaens:** *Satyr
and the Peasant,* ca.1620-21: p.19

MADRID:

Museo Nacional del Prado - Rubens: *The Three Graces,*
mid-1630s: p.8 - *Odorato,* 1617-18 (in collaboration with
Jan Brueghel I): p.19, 27 - *The Adoration of the Magi* (details):
p.13, 27, 31 - *Satyrs and Nymphs, allegory of Fertility* (details),
1636-38: p.27 - *The Rape of Europe* (according to Titian), about
1630: p.27- *The Garden of Love* (detail), ca.1634-35: p.31

MUNICH:

Alte Pinakothek - Rubens: *The Honeysuckle bower (Self-Portrait
with Isabelle Brandt),* ca.1609: p.14 - *Walk in the Antwerp
gardens* (detail), towards 1631: p.24 - *Helena Fourment in
Wedding Dress,* ca.1630 : p.24 - *Helena Fourment on the terrace
with her son Franz,* ca.1635 : p.25 - *Hippotamus and Crocodile
Hunt* (detail), 1615-16: p.27 - *Madonna and Child Garland of
Flowers and Putti,* ca.1618-20 (in collaboration with
Jan Brueghel I): p.31 - *Cupid adjusting his arc,* 1614 : p.31

VIENNA:

Kunsthistorisches Museum - Rubens: *The Head of Medusa*
(details painted by Snijders), ca.1617: p.26-27 - *The Four
Quarters of the Globe,* 1615-16: p.31- **Graphische
Sammlungen Albertina:** *Nicolas Rubens,* ca. 1625: p.25

VADUZ:

Sammlungen des Fürsten von Liechtenstein - Rubens: *Clara
Serena,* ca.1616 : p.25 - *Albert and Nicolas Rubens,* ca.1626: p.25

LONDON:

The National Gallery - Rubens: *Portrait of Susanna Fourment,*
ca.1622-25: cover, p.25 - *War and Peace* (detail), ca. 1629-30:
p.22, 27

ROME:

Pinacoteca Capitolina - Rubens: *Romulus and Remus* (detail),
1615-16: p.27 - **Michelangelo:** *The Sistine Chapel* (detail): p.6

PARIS:

Le Louvre - Rubens: *The Meeting of Marie de Medicis and
Henri IV at Lyons,* ca.1622-25: p.27-29,31

VENICE:

Titian: *The Assumption of the Holy Virgin,* 1516-18: p.7

Photo: *Charles Borromée church, Antwerp:* p.10

KMSKA- © Reproductiefonds Vlaamse Musea NV
Kathedraal Antwerpen - © Reproductiefonds Vlaamse
Musea NV
© Beeldarchief Collectie Antwerpen, Lowie De Peuter, Michel
Wuyts, Bart Huysmans
© KMSK, Brussel, Grafisch Buro Lefevre

Acknowledgements: Eric Vaes, Paul Huvenne, *Director KMSKA* and Marjolijn Barbier & Siska Beele, Liesbeth Wouters,
Conservator Rubenshuis and Nele Vervoort, Michel Draguet, *Director MRBAB* and Sabine van Sprang, *Conservator MRBAB* &
Nadia Ben Hamou, Renaud Gahide and Dirk Vandemeulebroecke, *Dexia Bank,* Pierre Waem, *De Kathedraal,* Timothy Naessens
and Dries Beheydt, *Lukas-Art in Flanders,* Bart Huysmans, *Beeldarchief Collectie Antwerpen,* Karel and Philippine van den Bergh,
Chloé Poucet, Priscilla d'Oultremont, Daniel de Duve, Corinne van Havre and all those who took part in the creation
of this book.